Where I Live/Donde Vivo

I Live in a Town/ Vivo en un pueblo

por Gini Holland

Reading consultant: Susan Nations, M.Ed., author/literacy coach/consultant

WEEKLY WR READER®
EARLY LEARNING LIBRARY

Please visit our web site at: www.earlyliteracy.cc
For a free color catalog describing Weekly Reader® Early Learning Library's
list of high-quality books, call 1-877-445-5824 (USA) or 1-800-387-3178 (Canada).
Weekly Reader® Early Learning Library's fax: (414) 336-0164.

Library of Congress Cataloging-in-Publication Data

Holland, Gini.
    [I live in a town. English & Spanish]
    I live in a town = Vivo en pueblo / Gini Holland.
      p. cm. — (Where I Live = Donde vivo)
    Includes bibliographical references and index.
    ISBN 0-8368-4131-X (lib. bdg.)
    ISBN 0-8368-4138-7 (softcover)
    1. Cities and towns—Juvenile literature. 2. City and town life—Juvenile literature.
  [1. Cities and towns. 2. City and town life. 3. Spanish language materials—Bilingual.]
  I. Title: Vivo en un pueblo. II. Title.
  HT152.H65   2004b
  307.76—dc22   2003064541

This edition first published in 2004 by
Weekly Reader® Early Learning Library
330 West Olive Street, Suite 100
Milwaukee, WI 53212 USA

Editor: JoAnn Early Macken
Picture research: Diane Laska-Swanke
Art direction and page layout: Tammy West
Photographer: Gregg Andersen

Printed in the United States of America

4 5 6 7 8 9 10 09 08 07 06

Note to Educators and Parents

Reading is such an exciting adventure for young children! They are beginning to integrate their oral language skills with written language. To encourage children along the path to early literacy, books must be colorful, engaging, and interesting; they should invite the young reader to explore both the print and the pictures.

Where I Live is a new series designed to help children read about everyday life in other places. In each book, young readers will learn interesting facts about different locations from the viewpoints of children who live there.

Each book is specially designed to support the young reader in the reading process. The familiar topics are appealing to young children and invite them to read — and re-read — again and again. The full-color photographs and enhanced text further support the student during the reading process.

In addition to serving as wonderful picture books in schools, libraries, homes, and other places where children learn to love reading, these books are specifically intended to be read within an instructional guided reading group. This small group setting allows beginning readers to work with a fluent adult model as they make meaning from the text. After children develop fluency with the text and content, the book can be read independently. Children and adults alike will find these books supportive, engaging, and fun!

Una nota a los educadores y a los padres

¡La lectura es una emocionante aventura para los niños! En esta etapa están comenzando a integrar su manejo del lenguaje oral con el lenguaje escrito. Para fomentar la lectura desde una temprana edad, los libros deben ser vistosos, atractivos e interesantes; deben invitar al joven lector a explorar tanto el texto como las ilustraciones.

Donde vivo es una nueva serie pensada para ayudar a los niños a conocer la vida cotidiana en distintos sitios. En cada libro, los jóvenes lectores conocerán datos interesantes acerca de lugares diferentes desde la perspectiva de los niños que viven allí.

Cada libro ha sido especialmente diseñado para facilitar el proceso de lectura. La familiaridad con los temas tratados atrae la atención de los niños y los invita a leer — y releer — una y otra vez. Las fotografías a todo color y el tipo de letra facilitan aún más al estudiante el proceso de lectura.

Además de servir como fantásticos libros ilustrados en la escuela, la biblioteca, el hogar y otros lugares donde los niños aprenden a amar la lectura, estos libros han sido concebidos específicamente para ser leídos en grupos de instrucción guiada. Este contexto de grupos pequeños permite que los niños que se inician en la lectura trabajen con un adulto cuya fluidez les sirve de modelo para comprender el texto. Una vez que se han familiarizado con el texto y el contenido, los niños pueden leer los libros por su cuenta. ¡Tanto niños como adultos encontrarán que estos libros son útiles, entretenidos y divertidos!

— Susan Nations, M.Ed., author, literacy coach,
and consultant in literacy development

I live in a town.

- - - - - - -

Vivo en un pueblo.

My town is small.

Mi pueblo es pequeño.

7

My town is near a farm.

Mi pueblo está cerca de una granja.

My town is near
the woods.

Mi pueblo está
cerca del
bosque.

I know all the people in my town.

En mi pueblo conozco a todo el mundo.

I swim in the pool in my town.

- - - - - - -

Nado en la piscina de mi pueblo.

I swing on the swings in the park.

- - - - - - -

Me mezo en los columpios del parque.

My town has
a big parade.

Mi pueblo
tiene un gran
desfile.

I like to live in a town.

Me gusta vivir en un pueblo.

Glossary/Glosario

farm — a plot of land where people raise animals and grow vegetables for food
granja — tierra donde se crían animales y se siembran vegetales para comer

parade — a march, usually with costumes and music, often to celebrate a holiday
desfile — marcha que se hace normalmente con disfraces y música para celebrar un día de fiesta

pool — a tank or body of water where people can swim
piscina — tanque o alberca donde se puede nadar

woods — a place where many trees grow close together
bosque — lugar donde crecen juntos muchos árboles

For More Information/Más información

Books/Libros

Casely, Judith. *On the Town: A Community Adventure*. New York: Greenwillow Books, 2002.

Geisert, Bonnie and Arthur. *Prairie Town*. Boston: Houghton Mifflin, 1999.

Hubbell, Patricia. *Sidewalk Trip*. New York: Harper Festival, 1999.

Scarry, Richard. *Richard Scarry's Busy, Busy Town*. Racine, Wis.: Western Publishing, 1994.

Web Sites/Páginas Web

Scavenger Hunt Scrapbook

www.planning.org/kidsandcommunity/scavenger_hunt/instructions.htm
Create a special book about your town

Index/Índice

About the Author/Información sobre la autora

Gini Holland is a writer and an editor. The author of over twenty nonfiction books for children, she was also a long-time educator for Milwaukee Public Schools, both in the elementary classroom and as a staff development instructor for both special education and general education teachers. She lives with her husband in Milwaukee, Wisconsin, and is a devoted fan of their son's two Chicago-based bands.

Gini Holland es escritora y editora. Es autora de más de 20 libros infantiles de temas realistas. Por muchos años fue maestra en el Sistema Escolar de Milwaukee tanto en las aulas de primaria como en los talleres de formación de los nuevos maestros y también en educación especial y formación profesional de los maestros. Vive con su esposo en Milwaukee, Wisconsin y es una decidida entusiasta de dos grupos musicales que su hijo tiene en Chicago.